WORD
CHO...

KIND WORDS ARE LIKE HONEY

SWEET TO THE SOUL AND
HEALTHY FOR THE BODY.

PROVERBS 16:24 (NLT)

ISBN: 978-1-7371659-2-7
First Edition June 2021
Words are like Honey : Bee Thankful
All rights reserved.

WORDSLIKEHONEY.COM

Open your arms as wide as you can to receive all the miracles with your name on them.

- SUZANNA THOMPSON

Next to excellence is the appreciation of it.

— WILLIAM MAKEPEACE THACKERY

Apppreciation is a wonderful thing: it makes what is excellent in others belong to us as well.

- VOLTAIRE

If we're too busy to enjoy and appreciate life, we're too busy.

— JEFF DANIELS

Never squander an opportunity to tell someone you love or appreciate them.

-KELLY ANN ROTHAUS

Life is not a race to be run, it's a journey to be savored every step of the way.

- KOBI YAMADA

Time is a very precious gift – so precious that it is only given to us moment by moment.

- AMELIA BARR

What a wonderful life I've had. I only wish I'd realized it sooner.

— SIDONIE GABRIELLE COLETTE

I always say to myself, what is the most important thing I can think about at this extraordinary moment?

— BUCKMINSTER FULLER

My heart gives thanks to empty moments given to dreams, and for thoughtful people who help those dreams come true.

— WILLIAM S. BRAITHWAITE

When life gives you a detour, enjoy and appreciate the scenery.

- MICHAEL NOLAN

I am learning what it means to be grateful. The more I think, the more I thank.

- UNKNOWN

The are two kinds of gratitude: The sudden kind we feel for what we take, the larger kind we feel for what we give.

– EDWIN ROBINSON

See, the good lying here. Seize it with a bold endeavor, happiness is always near.

— JOHANN WOLFGANG VON GOETHE

Remember that what you now have was once among the things you only hoped for.

- EPICURUS

Give thanks in all circumstances; for this is the will of God in Christ Jesus for you.

— 1 THESSALONIANS 5:18 NIV

When pursuing all you want, be sure to appreciate and enjoy all you have.

- JIM ROHN

The day, water, sun, moon, night – I do not have to purchase these things with money.

— PLAUTUS

Be grateful, truly grateful for one good friend or thoughtful person.

- SHAWNA CORLEY

My friends are my estate.

– EMILY DICKINSON

It's not how much we appreciate someone, it is how much they know it.

- ANDREW LYON

Say "thank you." You can't see it or touch it, but it goes straight to the heart.

- DAISY SAUNDERS

Appreciation
can make a day –
even change
a life.

- MARGARET COUSINS

One of God's greatest gifts to us are the people who love us.

- UNKNOWN

Celebrate your existence.

- WILLIAM BLAKE

Not what we say about our blessings, but how we use them, is the true measure of our appreciation.

- W.T. PURKISER

I love living. I have some problems with my life, but living is the best thing they've come up with so far.

- NEIL SIMON

Thanks for showing me that even on the darkest, rainiest days the sun is still there, just behind the clouds, waiting to shine again.

- LISA HARLOW

Life does not have
to be perfect to
be wonderful.

- ANNETTE FUNICELLO

Give thanks to the Lord, for he is good; his love endures forever.

- PSALM 118:1 NIV

Gratitude is the fairest blossom which springs from the soul.

- HENRY WARD BEECHER

Gratitude turns what we have into enough.

— ANONYMOUS

Gratitude is a powerful catalyst for happiness. It's the spark that lights a fire of joy in your soul.

— AMY COLLETTE

Thankfulness is the beginning of gratitude. Gratitude is the completion of thankfulness. Thankfulness may consist merely of words. gratitude is shown in acts.

- HENRI FREDERIC AMIEL

Happiness can not be travelled to, owned, earned, worn or consumed. Happiness is a spiritual experience of living every minute with love, grace and gratitude.

- DENIS WAITLEY

Joy is the simplest form of gratitude.

— KARL BARTH

In ordinary life, we hardly realize that we receive a great deal more than we give, and that it is only with gratitude that life becomes rich.

- DIETRICH BONHOEFFER

Gratitude is when memory is stored in the heart and not in the mind.

- LIONEL HAMPTON

What separates privilege from entitlement is gratitude.

— BRENÉ BROWN

Gratitude is riches.
Complaint is poverty.

— DORIS DAY

Be grateful for what you already have while you pursue your goals. If you aren't already grateful for what you have, what makes you think you would be happy with more.

ROY T. BENNETT

Nothing is more honorable than a grateful heart.

- LUCIUS ANNAEUS SENECA

If the only prayer you ever say in your entire life is thank you, it will be enough.

- MEISTER ECKHART

Feeling gratitude and not expressing it is like wrapping a present and not giving it.

— WILLIAM ARTUR WARD

Today I choose to live with gratitude for the love that fills my heart, the peace that rests within my spirit, and the voice of hope that says all things are possible.

— ANONYMOUS

As we express our gratitude, we must never forget that the highest appreciation is not to utter words, but to live by them.

- JOHN F. KENNEDY

Be thankful for what you have; you'll end up having more. If you concentrate on what you don't have, you'll never, ever have enough.

- OPRAH WINFREY

When I started counting my blessings, my whole life turned around.

— WILLIE NELSON

Gratitude is not only the greatest of virtues but the parent of all others.

- MARCUS TULLIUS CICERO

I would maintain that thanks are the highest form of thought, and that gratitude is happiness doubled by wonder.

- GILBERT C. CHESTERTON

We often take for granted the very things that deserve our gratitude.

- CYNTHIA OZICK

Gratitude is the sweetest thing in a seeker's life – in all human life. If there is gratitude in your heart, then there will be tremendous sweetness in your eyes.

– SRI CHINMOY

The more grateful I am, the more beauty I see.

- MARY DAVIS

There is a calmness to life lived with gratitude.

– RALPH H. BLUM

Gratitude is the most exquisite form of courtesy.

- JACQUE MARITAIN

The root of joy is gratefulness.

- DAVID STEINDL-RAST

I've had a remarkable life. I seem to be in such good places at the right time. You know, if you were to ask me to sum my life up in one word, gratitude.

- DIETRICH BONHOEFFER

Gratitude unlocks the fullness of life. It turns what we have into enough, and more. It turns denial into acceptance, chaos to order, confusion to clarity. It can turn a meal into a feast, a house into a home, a stranger into a friend.

- MELODY BEATTIE

Made in the USA
Monee, IL
11 June 2021